SELF-DEVELOPMENT FOR
EARLY YEARS MANAGERS

Related titles of interest:

Baby and Toddler Development Made Real
Sandy Green (1-84312-033-X)

Essential Skills for Managers of Child-Centred Settings
Emma Isles-Buck and Shelly Newstead (1-84312-034-8)

Planning an Appropriate Curriculum for the Under Fives
Rosemary Rodger (1-85346-912-2)

Planning Children's Play and Learning in the Foundation Stage
Jane Drake (1-85346-752-9)

Other titles in the same series:

Managing People and Teams
Chris Ashman and Sandy Green (1-84312-198-0)

Planning, Doing and Reviewing
Chris Ashman and Sandy Green (1-84312-199-9)

Managing Environment and Resources
Chris Ashman and Sandy Green (1-84312-200-6)

SELF-DEVELOPMENT FOR EARLY YEARS MANAGERS

Chris Ashman and Sandy Green

Illustrations by Dawn Vince

 David Fulton Publishers

David Fulton Publishers Ltd
The Chiswick Centre, 414 Chiswick High Road, London W4 5TF

www.fultonpublishers.co.uk

First published in Great Britain in 2004 by David Fulton Publishers
10 9 8 7 6 5 4 3 2 1

Note: The right of the authors to be identified as the authors of this work
has been asserted by them in accordance with the Copyright, Designs and
Patents Act 1988.

David Fulton Publishers is a division of Granada Learning Limited, part of ITV
plc.

Copyright © Chris Ashman and Sandy Green 2004

British Library Cataloguing in Publication Data
A catalogue record for this book is available from the British Library.

ISBN 1 84312 197 2

Typeset by Mark Heslington, Northallerton, North Yorkshire
Printed and bound in Great Britain

CONTENTS

ACKNOWLEDGEMENTS

The support and advice of Sandy has been invaluable in helping me to relate the ideas and thoughts of management to the complex world of Early Years provision. Many of the students I have worked with over the past ten years at Norton Radstock College have also helped me to learn so much.

Learning from the work of managers and practitioners of Little Learners nursery over the past years has also been key to my understanding.

I rely on the personal support and encouragement of Gina and the continued strength from my parents, thank you.

Chris Ashman

As always I have received encouragement and support from my husband John, who tirelessly listens to manuscripts and offers useful suggestions.

It has also been a pleasure to work with and support Chris throughout this series, having benefitted personally from his excellent management skills when we worked together in the past.

Sandy Green

Chapter 1

I AM A MANAGER

This chapter covers:

- An introduction to the role of a manager in Early Years
- An overview of some important management theory
- Some useful definitions and models to support your development

---

SCENARIO CASE STUDY

'What do you do, then?'

I felt excited and nervous as I went into the room. I was dreading the training session's 'warm-up'.

I always feel like my throat is drying up when I'm waiting my turn to introduce myself and say what I do. I try to listen to what the person next to me is saying and just about hear the trainer say to me, 'Tell us about your new job. It sounds very interesting.'

How will I answer the question?

How would you answer?

TO BE A MANAGER

Being a manager in the Early Years sector is a rewarding and demanding role. Many people, however, take some time to describe themselves as a manager who works within childcare. It may feel more comfortable to consider being a qualified practitioner who happens to be a manager.

The importance of being a manager

Every Early Years setting wants good management, clear direction, an appropriate curriculum, support for staff, good communication with parents, sound finances and a safe environment. When these things are in place the setting can demonstrate consistent good practice and will enjoy positive inspection reports, a good reputation and a bright future.

All managers will want to have a good staff team. Most will say that having good staff is the most important thing for a successful service and happy, thriving children.

The importance of the manager's role in finding, developing and shaping any group of staff is crucial. Without a good manager, staff will find it very difficult to maintain high standards. A fact to face is that within Early Years settings (and probably in all other settings) the absence of good management results in poor or no clear direction, an inconsistent approach to curriculum delivery, stagnating staff, dissatisfied complainants, inefficiency and risk.

You are a manager. Your team needs good management. Your skills will be required to develop yourself as a specialist manager in your setting.

Management prejudice

Some people think that managers are:

❏ The ones who sit in the office drinking coffee and chatting

❏ *The* decision-makers

❏ People who can take an easy situation and turn it into a complicated mess

❏ More likely to say 'No' than 'Yes'

❏ Former childcarers who have forgotten what the job is all about.

ACTIVITY 1.1

Think of a good manager you have known. For example, your first manager; the best manager you have known from your placements or work; or maybe someone from outside of childcare. Write a list of the things that you believe make them a good manager. Give yourself one minute to identify as many ideas as you can.

Things I believe make a manager good include:

_____

_____

_____

_____

Now think about the things that you link with poor management. Again give yourself one minute to write ideas in a list.

Things I believe make a manager poor include:

_____

_____

_____

_____

Comment

Your lists may include characteristics that are general points or some that are of special importance to you. Ideas that you may have identified could include:

'good' managers

✔ Honest
✔ Good communicators
✔ Child-centred
✔ Pay my wages on time
✔ Listen to other people

'bad' managers

✘ Manipulate people
✘ Are unclear or mislead
✘ Forget about the children
✘ Don't provide enough resources
✘ Don't ask for ideas

Your personal view about what makes a good manager, and a bad manager, is important to recognise. Consider which of your lists is longer and which was easier to draw up. Your answers may help you to clarify your personal beliefs.

The view you hold will influence how you wish to develop as a manager. This may well have been created from your experience but could benefit further from development of your understanding of management theory. Understanding your own value judgements and expectations will be helpful in your own progress as a manager. It will put into a context what you are aiming

GOOD OR BAD MANAGER ?

MANAGERS NEED FEEDBACK

to achieve. Your understanding will also help you to listen constructively to the feedback you get about your management performance. If you are not ready to listen constructively then stop now and reconsider your options. If your staff team doesn't give you feedback, then the parents probably will and the children will certainly let you know!

Learn by doing – and then do it again

Most people who become good managers do so through a mixture of increasing the number of times they do the 'right' things and minimising the times they take the 'wrong' action. As with all learning you will make mistakes. In fact you need to identify mistakes so that you can find a better way to manage in the future.

A BRIEF GUIDE TO SOME MANAGEMENT THEORY

Understanding some of the main themes and changes of emphasis in management theory over the twentieth century will put your Early Years management into a useful context for present challenges. It can also help to understand that there are various ways of addressing an issue.

Natural selection of leaders

As the late Victorians were coming to terms with Darwin's theory of natural selection in the evolution of life on earth, the widely held belief was that leaders were 'born not made'.

Origins of this view can be traced from the ancient concept of kings being born to rule, appointed by God.

FOLLOWING THE LEADER

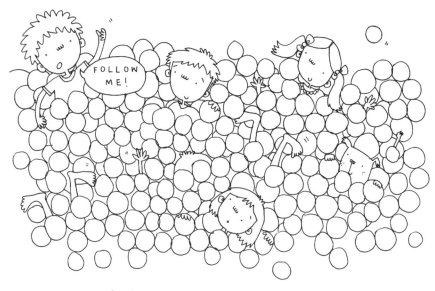

EMERGING FROM THE GROUP

It was adapted to fit more democratic political circumstances by the expectation that the best leaders would emerge from the group as a result of their natural abilities. This can be illustrated by the saying that 'the cream always rises to the top'.

History provides many examples that seem to justify this approach – Joan of Arc, Gandhi, Churchill, Martin Luther King. These people, so this theory goes, were successful leaders because they possessed the skills and characteristics required for their time and circumstances. Such 'natural leaders' were often part of a social or political group that helped them, through opportunities or access to other people and resources.

This belief in natural leadership did not find favour in a modern meritocracy. The belief emerged that anyone can achieve a position of leadership and responsibility within society regardless of their birth circumstances, their family or cultural background, or their family wealth. Leadership positions can be achieved through the development of skills, the application of experience, and the taking of chances.

It's not about destiny and birth so much as opportunity, determination and application.

Scientific management

As industrialists developed mass production techniques, the era of the heroic leader was replaced by that of the efficient manager. The responsibility of management was to take the separate parts – labour (workers) and capital (raw materials and equipment) – and create something new. This new thing (the product) was worth more than the sum of the parts and so wealth was created and added.

One well-known pioneer of this scientific approach to management was the American engineer Frederick

WHERE THERE'S MUCK THERE'S BRASS

Taylor. A Quaker by religion, Taylor was determined to organise complex work into a series of simpler activities in which workers could specialise. Rather than expecting people to be able to work at all parts of the production process, workers were trained to become highly skilled in their specialist activity and work together. The group was reliant on everyone doing their part.

Within Early Years settings we do this too, in that we train staff to be experts in some areas, for example, keyworker for a specific child, or child protection nominee.

Unlike earlier capitalists who had seen the workers more as 'units of production' – something to get the most out of for the least cost – Taylor was partially driven by the desire for workers to benefit from the additional wealth created. His workers were paid higher wages than others.

Some Early Years providers offer their staff an attractive package of salary, working conditions and reduced-cost places for their own children. These 'perks' fit in with Taylor's ethos in that they try to attract and retain the best staff available locally.

Operational management

Another significant development in the theory of management has been attributed to the French industrialist Henri Fayol. Through his observations of industrial practice Fayol identified 14 principles of management. These principles, he suggested, can apply to many aspects of life other than business, for example politics, and philanthropic or charity works.

Fayol's 14 Principles of Management

Fayol's 14 principles	Applied examples for Early Years
❏ Division of work	efficient allocation and specific roles, for example Child Protection, key worker for individual children
❏ Authority and responsibility	the job title and the person where there are named staff who are qualified status Practitioners, or team leaders, or managers
❏ Discipline	respect for agreements made, such as rotas or work objectives that have been agreed are put into practice
❏ Unity of command	clear instruction from one manager. There is clear understanding of who can authorise what type of decision
❏ Unity of direction	clear reason for the instruction, actions based upon best child focused approach
❏ Subordination of the individual	for the benefit of the whole team. An example is where all staff members are aware of the need to maintain the service when requesting things for themselves
❏ Remuneration	payment should be fair, that pay rates should be based upon known and understood criteria
❏ Centralisation	decisions made at the best point, such as practitioners are clear about the level of decision-making they have within their work with the children
❏ Scalar chain	management hierarchy should not stop decision-making, the system does not prevent a timely decision being made
❏ Order	clarity of role and purpose, everyone in the team knows the broad roles of other colleagues
❏ Equity	by managers to gain loyalty, in that managers do not demonstrate favouritism to any staff
❏ Stability of tenure	loyalty by managers to their workers, where the manager balances business considerations with staff needs such as annual leave
❏ Initiative	thinking, planning and acting. An example is that the service is forward thinking and not solely reactive
❏ Esprit de corps	teamwork, that value is placed upon helping and supporting team members

ACTIVITY 1.2

Think about an Early Years setting familiar to you. Identify an example for as many of Fayol's 14 principles as you can.

Division of work
Authority and responsibility
Discipline
Unity of command
Unity of direction
Subordination of the individual
Remuneration
Centralisation
Scalar chain
Order
Equity
Stability of tenure
Initiative
Esprit de corps

Behavioural sciences

During the same period that scientific management was being developed other managers were exploring the impact of people and their behaviour upon work settings.

The developing discipline of psychology fuelled research[1] and helped to generate new ideas that were applied to management theory. The work of Elton Mayo *et al.* and Frederick Herzberg are two major

[1] For example, Lillian Gilbreth, 'Psychology of Management' (1914), cited in Koontz and Weihrich 1988, p. 34.

contributions to the behavioural sciences view of management. Their work can be applied to many sectors. It particularly suits service industries that are heavily dependent upon staff, such as in Early Years provision.

Mayo
One of the most famous and influential examples of this work was the *Hawthorn Studies*.[2] The main purpose of the study was to measure the effect of working conditions upon the productivity of employees.

ACTIVITY 1.3

Think about a staff team that you are familiar with.

Note your ideas to answer these two questions.

1. What would you expect to happen if their working conditions were improved?
2. What would you expect if working conditions were made worse?

The range of working conditions that you might consider could include salary, incentives or rewards for achieving targets, the working environment, available equipment and resources.

Think in terms of the amount and quality of the work produced.

_____

_____

_____

_____

_____

[2] Mayo, Roethlisberger *et al.*, cited in Koontz and Weihrich 1988, pp. 34–6.

Comment

Depending upon your personal values about what motivates people you may have drawn conclusions that lie between extremes of:

'Improved working conditions will motivate staff to work harder and produce improved quality. Inferior conditions would demotivate staff and work rates will fall, along with the quality.'

'Improved working conditions will make staff feel too comfortable. It will encourage them to be greedy for more and any improvement in their work will be short-lived. Inferior conditions will show them that the business needs all the effort it can get from them. There is no room for luxury.'

Within the Hawthorn Studies, which were based in a manufacturing production line, the working hypothesis was that improved working conditions would improve productivity.

In the first of the series of experiments two groups of workers were chosen. For one group the working environment was improved by providing better lighting in the factory. The second group had the same lighting as usual.

As expected the first group's productivity increased. They produced more work than they had before the changes.

The surprise came when the productivity of the second group was measured during the experiment. It had also increased.

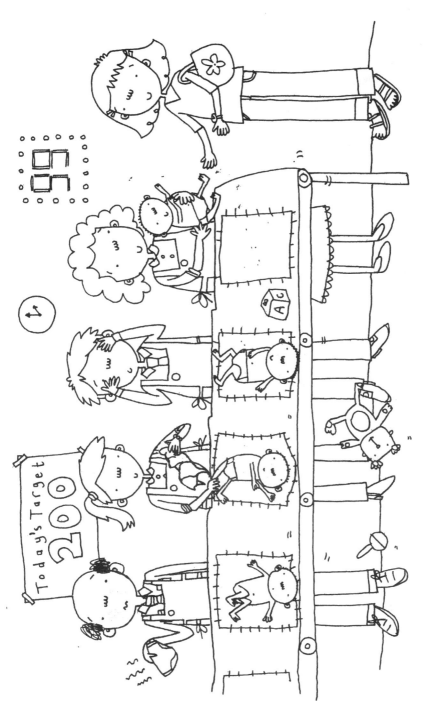

MOTIVATING THE WORKERS: IDEA NUMBER ONE

ACTIVITY 1.4

What ideas can you think of that could explain the increase in productivity in the second group?

_____

_____

The series of experiments went on for years in the 1920s and 1930s. Each time the researchers tried different changes to see if they could find the combination of things that triggered improved productivity. The striking thing was that even when working conditions were normal, or were even made worse, productivity improved compared with the rest of the factory.

It was a puzzle to identify what could be causing workers to become more productive, even when they were put in relatively poor working environments.

The conclusions drawn from this work challenged some of the logical scientific approaches to management. It seemed to be more complex than just expecting to gain increased productivity as a result of training and equipping workers for specialist roles.

It appeared that a number of factors resulted in positive outcomes. Examples include:

- being selected as part of the experiment and so feeling special
- being consulted and asked about opinions and feelings
- being challenged with a demanding and interesting task

- being trained
- recognising individuals as part of a team
- receiving feedback on both performance and contribution.

ACTIVITY 1.5

Can you think of an example where, despite worse environmental conditions, a group of people have worked well in a team? Examples could possibly come from your own experience, from history or from sport.

_____

_____

_____

Comment

The sporting world has many examples where a team has been strengthened by the hardships they face, or the perception that 'everyone is against them'.

Sports coaches often use this mental model to bond a group together 'against the world'. In Early Years the same phenomena could come about as a result of poor publicity, or criticism from outside the team.

Political, especially military, examples abound where from the expected short-term defeat a victory has been won. For example, the Alamo galvanised a successful fight for Texan independence; the Dunkirk evacuation was an inspirational turning-point towards the Allied victory in the Second World War.

SCENARIO CASE STUDY

The White Rabbit pre-school meets in a shabby village hall that is safe but in a bad state of repair. They are not allowed to put anything on the walls (village committee rule number 7!), or leave anything out after the session as the hall is used for other activities.

The staff work hard to be ready when the children arrive. They transform the drab, bare hall with pictures and paintings hung from screens and window catches.

They are determined, as a team, to provide a bright and stimulating environment for the children, despite the conditions and restrictions they are faced with.

Herzberg

What a manager does will affect the motivation of individuals and teams. Many managers spend large amounts of time and effort trying to keep their team's motivation high. How much of this time and effort is used effectively is worth questioning.

Some management theory explores assumptions that these types of things really do result in high levels of motivation and job satisfaction.

The work of Herzberg[3] identified two different types of factors that led to job satisfaction. One type, when present, resulted in increased satisfaction among employees. These he called 'motivators'. Examples of such include achievement, recognition and responsibility.

[3] Frederick Herzberg, 'Motivation and Maintenance', Chapter 12 in Kennedy 1991.

HOW (NOT) TO MOTIVATE THE WORKERS: IDEA NUMBER TWO

ACTIVITY 1.6

Make a list of things that you believe improve motivation of staff.

_____

_____

_____

_____

_____

_____

Comment

Many people will identify things that people *talk* about as being high-level motivators. These often include:

❑ high salary
❑ pay rises
❑ more holidays
❑ bonus payments or perks.

The second type had no real positive effect on satis-faction levels when present, but when absent caused dissatisfaction. These he called 'hygiene' factors. The word 'hygiene' is used to acknowledge important factors that only become apparent when they are not working well. For example, when hygiene is poor we are aware it is poor through various senses. In management, 'policy or working conditions' can be viewed as a hygiene motivator for staff. You may have experience of having to work in a poor environment – too cold or hot, the wrong levels of light or noise – or

WHAT DO STAFF HAVE TO DO BEFORE THEIR MANAGER LISTENS?

WHAT IS THE JOB ABOUT?

where you were expected to complete long and seemingly pointless bureaucracy:

'You will need to fill in your name, address, date of birth and national insurance number again on this green form before I can process your application.'

Not many managers are thanked for their excellent policies and procedures, although plenty are criticised for having none or poorly thought-out procedures. Many are criticised for installing yet more, seemingly pointless bureaucracy that 'stops me working with the children'.

Salary levels are often quoted as motivators. This model of management theory identifies only a short-term improvement in motivation resulting from salary increases. It appears that salary level is important in attracting the right staff to apply for the job. It is limited as a tool to maintain long-term motivational increases.

GETTING THE BALANCE RIGHT

In summary, Herzberg's work sets out hygiene factors as having the ability to demotivate if they do not exist or fail to satisfy the expectations or needs of staff.

In order that managers can make a positive impact on motivation they need to find ways of providing 'job enrichment'. These can include the existence of challenging and meaningful work, achievement, recognition and development in the job role. If these factors exist then sustained levels of motivation and job satisfaction can also follow.

DEFINITIONS AND MODELS FOR EARLY YEARS

Managing

Who is a manager within an Early Years setting? A simple question, but one with a whole range of possible answers.

Most staff within childcare do some work and take some responsibility that could be called management.

ACTIVITY 1.7

For each of these statements write an example from the viewpoint of a Level 3 practitioner.

❑ I supervise others in their activities

_____

_____

❑ I am responsible for planning

_____

_____

❏ I have to review how well things went

_____

_____

❏ I gather the things needed to complete a piece of work

_____

_____

❏ If things are going wrong I put them right

_____

_____

Could you also find examples for the work of a supervisor, a deputy, a Level 2 practitioner? The work of Early Years practitioners always includes some aspects of management. By the nature of caring for children a degree of responsibility is involved. That is one reason why qualified status is set at NVQ Level 3 (BTEC National/CACHE Diploma).

It is an intrinsic factor of the work; childcarers are responsible not only for themselves but also for others.

This responsibility can be illustrated simply in the following diagram.

PLAN → IMPLEMENT → REVIEW

This model can then be applied to the Early Years curriculum, risk assessments for health & safety, finance & budgets, team-building or other management activities. While the model seems very simple (almost too simple?) the failure to carry out the three stages fully can result in 'good managers' failing to keep their practice consistently good. Some managers get stuck at the 'plan' stage. Others rush, unplanned, into action too quickly.

Being a manager means more

If most staff in Early Years undertake some responsibilities that can be described as management, what then makes a manager different?

SCENARIO CASE STUDY

At Little Ducklings nursery everyone has his or her role and responsibilities. Hannah is responsible for planning, Rashid supervises student placement procedures, Donna plans the parent newsletter and Meera oversees displays and the notice board.

They are all Level 3 practitioners and clearly have management roles.

Stephanie is the nursery manager. Her role is different from the other staff.

The range of responsibilities held by managers is wider than for the people they manage. A supervisor is responsible for their team's work and perhaps other specific functions within the service to children and parents (e.g. the newsletter). The manager is responsible for the whole service, the whole staff team. This responsibility includes legal aspects as well as those imposed by organisation or business.

Below is a list of activities and responsibilities that you may expect to be included in a description of good management.

❑ Doing things efficiently and effectively
❑ Getting the job done through other people
❑ Organising teams and allocating resources
❑ Counting the cost of things
❑ Knowing the value of activities with children
❑ Finding the right people to join as new staff
❑ Checking to ensure that children and parents get a good service
❑ Helping team members to develop their skills and awareness
❑ Making sure of financial security for the future
❑ Dealing with 'difficult' things.

Manager and leader

The words 'manager' and 'leader' are often used in an interchangeable way. It seems that for many people they mean the same. There are differences, however.

The ideas outlined above relate to the manager's role. It seems a reasonable working definition to say that

Management is the responsibility to do things in the most efficient and effective ways, to get the best in the present.

Leadership is the responsibility to consider what changes are needed to be taken now to be in the best situation for the future, to think about the future.

Leaders are identifiable in most groups. Although this is more of an art than a science, the role of a leader can often include some of the following:

❑ Having a specialist skill or knowledge
❑ Being a facilitator, getting the best out of others
❑ Being visionary or inspirational
❑ Having high energy or spreading enthusiasm
❑ Being persistent, not giving up.

When you work with children you may have noticed those who take a lead. They may be the ones who suggest ideas, organise things or other people, and find resources. Some may be great communicators, they might look after other children and be aware of feelings, show empathy and understanding. Some can enforce the rules or cajole others into action or conformity.

When there is a clear leader there is still the issue of whether other children will follow. Some will, others may not.

Compare this with your experience of adults within an Early Years setting. One difference will be the positional power of the job role. You are a manager, and with that title comes some degree of intrinsic influence and power. It may not always feel like you have more power, or more decision-making influence, than other team members.

Adair's model

John Adair has developed one very useful model of management.[4] There are three main areas of concern

---

[4] John Adair, Chapter 1 in Kennedy 1991.

for any manager – the task, the individuals and the team.

The *task* is the service or activity that the business exists to perform. The *individual* relates to individual staff members of any group formed to perform the task. The *team* is the whole group with all the tensions or dynamics surrounding them.

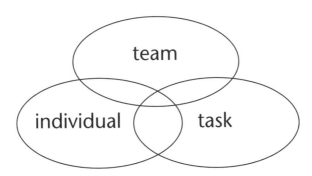

There are overlaps between the three areas of concern. Each has an importance and at times a high priority. If any one area is left unattended the overall well-being of the service will suffer. As a manager you will spend time ministering to each, but will need to keep all three in mind.

For Early Years managers the *task* can be anything from the delivery of the overall service, to a specific activity such as 'planning the curriculum for the next six weeks'.

The *individual* may be about the development, performance or support needs of any one person in the team.

Team concerns can include developing better under-standing, finding new staff to complement the existing skills mix, or resolving tensions between people.

SCENARIO CASE STUDY

During one week at Greystones nursery the manager had to be aware of the following:

❑ *Gathering together evidence for the quality assurance application (task)*
❑ *Finding time to support a member of staff in the final preparation of her NVQ folder (individual)*
❑ *Sorting out the staff annual rota to accommodate changes in staff roles (team).*

This model may be easier to understand if you imagine the old party game of spinning plates on sticks! Each plate is set spinning on top of a stick or cane. By twizzling a cane you can maintain the plate on its top spinning successfully.

PAYING ATTENTION

Each plate needs attention at the right time. Failure to twizzle the cane (or attend to the area of concern) at the right time will result in that plate wobbling. A wobbling plate can cause us to panic. Sometimes we may be tempted to over-twizzle in an effort to compensate for the lack of earlier attention! The risk of a wobble turning into a falling plate can be increased by either further lack of attention or over-attention.

As Early Years managers we want to minimise the wobblers by twizzling at the right time by the correct amount.

This party game is not easy. In fact you need to be skilled to even get the plates spinning in the first place. Likewise, for a manager this model is not as easy to implement as it is to understand.

ACTIVITY 1.8

It can be useful to reflect upon your own experience as a manager (or of being managed). Estimate how much time over the past month you (or your manager) have spent on

% of working hours

1. the task
2. the team
3. individuals

If you do not know, especially if you are the manager, then it will be useful to keep a diary record of your activities over the next two weeks.

Ask yourself, 'Am I spending the appropriate amount of time on each of the three areas?'

> **Comment**
>
> Many managers find that they spend more time and energy on individual staff (or an individual member of staff) than they think they should! This may be because the management of people is a complex and time-consuming activity, if done well.

NVQ model

The NVQ (National Vocational Qualification) in Early Years Care and Education provides an approved and substantial framework for managers. It is a very different model to Adair's work, being based upon nationally agreed standards and forming the core of assessed vocationally specific qualifications.

There are different levels of the framework that may be more relevant to managers in different settings. The Level 4 (professional updating) guidance targets those managers who are responsible for the organisation and running of an Early Years service, including the work of other staff and some of the business responsibilities.

If you undertake an NVQ qualification you need to provide evidence of your skills and knowledge against the required standards.

The Level 4 framework provides standards, in the form of units, that are mandatory for managers to demonstrate their competence against:

❑ Access, review and update your own knowledge of significant and emerging theory and practice
❑ Develop your own resources
❑ Provide information to support decision-making.

There are four other groups of units that candidates can select from. These option groups are:

❏ Management – where your practical management of an Early Years setting can be underpinned and developed. Unit topics include:
   ❏ child health, safety and protection
   ❏ curriculum
   ❏ relationships with parents
   ❏ performance of teams and individuals
   ❏ development and implementation of policies
❏ Enhancing quality and quality control – where the focus is on the role of supporting other services to maintain and improve on the required standards of Early Years provision.
❏ Advanced practice – especially for staff who wish to specialise further in Early Years provision at Level 4.
❏ General – offers a range of other choices that may interest candidates and that are relevant to both good practice and good management in the sector.

The NVQ framework provides a clear set of responsibilities and functions for managers in Early Years to use. Demonstration of competence against the criteria can lead to achievement of a qualification once this evidence is assessed through an NVQ centre. Alternatively the framework provides an ideal model for managers wishing to plan and review their Continued Professional Development.

REVIEW OF 'I AM A MANAGER'

This chapter has helped you if you can

✓ Explain the role of a manager in terms of the difference from being a practitioner
✓ Outline some of your core values that will influence you as a manager
✓ Describe some main characteristics of scientific, operational and behavioural approaches to management
✓ Apply some of your experiences to a model of management.

References and suggested further reading

K. Blanchard, P. Zigarmi and D. Zigarmi (1990) *Leadership and the One Minute Manager*, Fontana.
C. Kennedy (1991) *Guide to the Management Gurus*, Century Business.
H. Koontz and H. Weihrich (1988) *Management*, 9th edn, McGraw-Hill.

Websites

www.comp.glam.ac.uk/teaching/ismanagement/manstyles1f.htm (brief introductions to many different management theories)
www.teambuilding.co.uk/john_adair

Chapter 2

FROM COLLEAGUE TO BOSS

This chapter covers:

- How to explore the sort of manager you want to be
- Support and mentoring to help you develop
- The impact and expectations of other people on your management
- Moving towards the practice of management

THINK LIKE A MANAGER

What sort of a manager are you?

This is a simple enough question to ask yourself. For many people it is a question that can provoke a complex or confused answer.

This chapter will provide you with a range of ways to consider your understanding of the manager's role, along with activities designed to help you in your reflective development.

How to 'think like a manager'

> 'The roles and responsibilities of a manager are different from those of other Early Years team members.'

If you accept this assertion then it follows that people who take on a managerial role need to acknowledge themselves as a manager. They also need to be accepted by other team members as a manager.

This may seem obvious. Many managers, however, will feel the temptation to dilute this truth. They view themselves as the team's representative or the one who organises things ('it could be any of us'). For a manager in such a state of mind the transition from colleague to boss, or from team member to team leader, is still a difficult process they have yet to complete.

Self-image and expectations of work-related responsibilities have to change to enable a successful transition from colleague to boss. Being aware of your self-image is a good start to 'thinking like a manager'.

ACTIVITY 2.1

Complete the following sentence with your own ideas.

As an Early Years practitioner my strengths include ... (e.g. being focused on the needs of children as individuals.)

_____

_____

_____

As an Early Years manager my strengths include ... (e.g. organising team members' duties in an efficient way.)

_____

_____

_____

Comment

Compare your two lists. Which list was easier to complete? Do you have about the same number of ideas? How would you rate the weighting of the ideas – which one is more important?

What conclusions can you draw about your self-image with these roles?

SCENARIO CASE STUDY

Sonia is good at organising things. She motivates others to join her and gives them clear guidance. She interacts well with children at levels appropriate to each of them. Sonia is interested in special educational needs and wants to find out more, so she has booked to go on a course.

Sonia is approachable and ensures that she is available to both parents and staff when they need her. Her communication skills and practice are both excellent.

Some of Sonia's strengths are those of a practitioner and some are those of a manager. Think through which are which.

If you are still unsure try this:

ACTIVITY 2.2

Think about a range of Early Years practitioners you have known. Especially think about their strengths and weaknesses. With these thoughts in mind finish this sentence (or better still write a short paragraph).

As a manager of Early Years practitioners I believe most members of staff to display characteristics of being...

_____

_____

_____

_____

Comment

The more you write the easier it should be to reflect on some of your core values (principles and rules that you hold that will affect your actions as a manager).

Two different ways of completing the sentence would be to characterise staff as being:

| X | or | Y |

X	Y
• Committed	• Belligerent
• Positive	• Negative
• Hard working	• Self-centred
• Child-centred	• Selfish
• Teamworkers	• Unskilled
• Highly skilled	• Resistant to change
• Continually developing	• Only seeing problems
• Self-motivated	• Motivated by threats

Theory X or Y is taken from the work of Douglas McGregor.[1] He believed that how a manager works will be based upon how they view human nature and their relationship with the staff they manage. It can be useful to check your assumptions against the X and Y extremes. Which list more closely matches your own working assumptions? Your views may be influenced by an experience of working with a great team, or you may be unfortunate to know of an awful set-up.

Whatever your experience, it is useful to identify why a team is 'great' or 'awful'. As the manager you have a huge influence on any group of staff.

As manager you have an even larger responsibility to maintain and develop the positive characteristics and address the negatives.

INTRODUCING MS X AND MS Y

[1] Douglas McGregor, 'Theory X and Theory Y', Chapter 19 in Kennedy 1991.

SCENARIO CASE STUDY

Daisy Chain nursery is having a crisis morning.

It is a Wednesday. Two staff members have phoned in to report sickness, as have a number of children's parents. A virus seems to have hit the baby and toddler unit.

The parent of one child still attending nursery demands to know what measures are going to be taken to help prevent further cross-infection.

The manager, Julie, notices that Justine, who is playing with play dough, and Rosie, playing with the doll's house, are looking pale and appear unusually quiet. She hopes that they are not going down with the same virus.

Julie does not usually spend any specific time in the nursery rooms on a Wednesday. She usually catches up on paperwork. Today she was planning to get to grips with writing up those nursery planned actions that were agreed following the recent Ofsted inspection. These included an identified need to better plan the use of the outdoor play space and improved communication with parents.

Julie also needs to plan the next staff rota and write up her notes for a student on placement who attends Thursdays and Fridays. The student's tutor is visiting tomorrow.

With all these pressures Julie thinks about moving staff around to ensure that the correct adult:child ratio is maintained at all times. She is aware, however, that this may cause some distress for two children who are just settling in and are quite dependent on specific staff members. Some of the staff are grumbling about the situation and have reminded Julie that it is hard to cope with two staff absent.

ACTIVITY 2.3

Think through the scenario case study and identify some options that Julie could choose from. Consider what the priorities are:

1. from the viewpoint of an Early Years practitioner
2. from the viewpoint of the manager
3. for the needs of the children.

Comment

Sometimes a manager has to make choices that will not please everyone, including himself or herself. Depending upon your core values and the assumptions you have made about the other team members you may have chosen from a range of solutions to this challenge. It matters that you consider the options and weigh up the costs and benefits to the children, staff, parents and yourself.

So, I've got to be good at everything!

Many developing managers will catch themselves uttering the phrase, 'I wouldn't ask any of my team to do something that I couldn't do.'

This is, from one perspective, a lovely sentiment. It is full of team spirit and remembering your roots. It could mean (or be interpreted by others to mean) that you wouldn't put staff in a situation that their experience, training and skills couldn't deal with; it could mean that you will take a share of the 'tough' jobs.

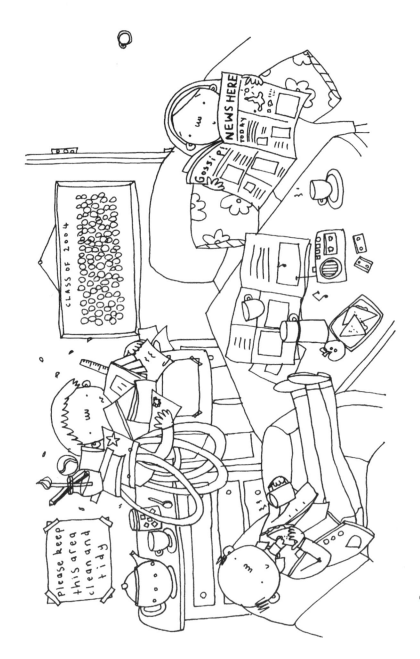

SOMETIMES THE SMART THING TO DO IS SHARE

From another perspective this statement holds some fundamental flaws for your service, for the children in your care and for the staff team within your responsibility. For example, it might mean that you won't let anyone in your team become seen as more of an expert than you. It could indicate that you will spend precious management time and energy undertaking tasks that other staff could (should) do.

SCENARIO CASE STUDY

Jan is the manager of Sunnymeades crèche. When a child's parents ask for advice on the special educational needs code of practice, Jan does not hesitate to refer them to Dasmani, who is the SENCO for the setting. Dasmani has a greater level of expertise and training in this area of Early Years practice.

'I don't have to be the best Early Years practitioner in my team.'

Try saying it – to yourself – out loud.

It may feel strange, especially if you are reading this in a public place and have just shouted out this assertion to a shocked audience, but hopefully it is also a relief.

Your job is to be as good a manager as you can be. For the children in the care of your service, for their parents your customers, and for your team, your priority is to be a good manager.

As a working manager you will probably still be included in direct childcare activities. It is desirable to continue to do so. Your thinking, however, needs to be able to move from a focus upon your practitioner role to that of your management role. There are other practitioners, but you alone are the designated manager.

Find a friend

The role of an Early Years manager can feel a little lonely. The realisation that you are different from the rest of the team may be something you are already comfortable with – but many people take time to achieve such comfort.

If you still doubt that you are now something more than just 'one-of-the-gang' you could try asking members of your team what they expect of you. To support your managerial development use what your Early Years training was based upon – knowledge and reflective practice.

As a practitioner you will have had a whole range of colleagues to discuss things with, to explore ideas and

THE NEW GIRL

share concerns. As part of your managerial role you, through staff supervision, provide similar support to members of your staff team.

Who have you got to support you? Who can be your mentor?

Many managers will be able to identify someone within their team who they respect and could be a potential confidential supporter. This temptation should probably be avoided. However good and willing the person is, they are not in the right position to act as a mentor for you. This person may be a great mentor for someone else – either another member of the team, or even a manager in another setting, but not for you. What would, for instance, happen to your working relationship and credibility if they became the subject of a parent's allegation and you had to undertake a management investigation into their work? Part of being a good manager is to think about the future 'what if' scenarios and avoid situations where you can't win.

ACTIVITY 2.4

To help you identify potential mentors think about people who may be able to provide you with a reflective viewpoint that you need. Which of the following would you, as the manager, benefit from?

❏ Reassurance
❏ Challenges to rethink your decisions and actions
❏ Help for you to set new and demanding professional goals

❏ High expectations of your practice and development
❏ Help for you to identify and celebrate your successful achievements
❏ Asking you to focus on the 'big issues' of your job
❏ Bringing you back to practical details.

Comment

Identifying what you need from a mentor is very important. The next step is to think of as many people as you can who could potentially provide what you need. It is better to have more than one choice. This helps both you and the person who is your first choice in the event that they say 'No' or can't provide such support yet. It also indicates that this is a professional relationship that you seek, not an extension of friendship.

The mix of approaches that you benefit from when working with your mentor will probably change as your managerial career develops. The general use of mentoring as a sounding-board will be a great bolster at times when the job is at its toughest.

Networking is an anytime activity

For many managers finding a mentor is not easy. Early Years managers in other settings may be business or professional competitors; or the chance to meet up may be limited, rare or non-existent.

ACTIVITY 2.5

Here is a chance to demonstrate some 'thinking like a manager'.
  Who could act as a mentor for you?
  Some ideas to consider:

❑ A successful and experienced manager from a different sector
❑ A tutor or trainer involved in Early Years
❑ An Early Years manager who is far enough away, or whose service is different enough not be a competitor
❑ Someone you know who has training in active listening, e.g. counselling, keyworking
❑ Your local authority contacts, e.g. EYDCP (Early Years Development & Childcare Partnership)
❑ Yourself – if you can 'book quality time' away from other things and people to think through and evaluate your work.

Comment

You may be tempted to choose the final option, especially if it seems the easiest one. It is probably the hardest to follow up productively. If you doubt this try asking yourself or a friend which is more likely to happen – going to the fitness club or evening class if you go alone, or going if you have arranged to meet someone else there. For many people it will be the latter arrangement. To avoid letting others down we keep appointments with people more often than those we 'make' with ourselves.

TIME TO THINK CREATIVELY

Once you have identified people who could be your mentor be clear about the following things before you make your approach.

Be clear about:

❑ Your expectations. What is the role you expect your mentor to take? Be clear what you want from them in the initial stages of the mentoring relationship, and be ready to tell them.

❑ Seeking the expectations of your mentor. It may be that they have a fixed view of mentoring that differs from yours. Alternatively they may be interested in you helping them in some way.

❑ The probable length of this mentoring relationship.

❑ How the mentoring relationship will end. You and your mentor will need to know about the 'get-out clause'. This is important so that neither person feels trapped within the commitment.

Sample Mentoring Agreement

Name of mentor: _____
Name of mentee: _____
Date of agreement: ____/____/____
Main aims of the mentoring relationship:

Agreed methods (meetings' regularity, venue, length)

Review period: _____
Agreed method of concluding the arrangement

It would be quite reasonable to expect the person you approach to take a little time to consider the offer to be your mentor. They need to think about their ability to meet the time commitment, the professional role, and to make sure they are not saying 'yes' as a response to feeling flattered by being asked.

If the response is positive you may choose to discuss and agree a short written statement. This will clarify the arrangements and can really help both your mentor and you.

The act of writing a statement about this supportive relationship can reassure both of you of what it is that you are aiming to achieve.

How do I know when I'm 'thinking like a manager'?

You know that you need to think like a manager. You even have some ideas of how to develop an approach to doing the thinking. Next you need to find ways of 'catching yourself doing it'.

ACTIVITY 2.6

Think about yourself as a practising or potential Early Years manager. Below are some prompts for you to write descriptive statements about your views of yourself.

I have reflected on my current skills and knowledge as an Early Years manager and I believe the following things are relevant about me as a

Team leader:

_____

Curriculum planner:

_____

Problem-solver:

_____

Health & Safety enforcer:

_____

Planner for the service/business:

_____

Controller of the working environment:

_____

Guardian of the finances:

_____

Preparer for inspection:

_____

Comment

The activity suggests a range of managerial respon-sibilities across which you should be developing your skills and awareness. By reviewing your state-ments you will be able to identify areas where you are strong and areas that you wish to develop. There are other models that you could use to make self-assessment judgements, e.g. the NVQ Early Years framework.

In the next chapter you will be encouraged to think about what action to take to build on your strengths and address your weaknesses.

HOW OTHER PEOPLE SEE YOU

SCENARIO CASE STUDY

Charis has just been appointed manager of Peter Pan Nursery. She is really excited and has arranged a full staff meeting at the end of her first week.

After talking generally about the nursery and her first impressions and findings so far she thanks the staff for their support and patience. 'This may be Peter Pan Nursery but I know there is no Tinkerbell able to sprinkle me with magic dust. I have a lot to learn and I am still finding my way as a manager. I hope you will all continue to work with me as we develop together.'

Magic dust

Just one of the amazing things about being, or becoming, an Early Years manager is how other people view you in the role.

Team members who previously have been colleagues, workmates, sharers of news, views and moans, may change their behaviour almost overnight.

For many aspiring managers this prediction may not sound like a certainty. Your team mates may continue to treat you as they have previously done, even if your role as a manager is new. Probably for those people who take on a managerial role within an existing workplace the shift will be gradual. Be prepared, though, for it will happen.

TO OTHERS YOU LOOK LIKE A MANAGER

Of course this change in the working relationship is connected with your management role. There is often a quick shift in the expectation that other people have of you at work, in that they immediately expect you to know things like

✓ How the voucher scheme administration works
✓ When the next inspection is due
✓ What the rota is for Friday
✓ What to do about Joanne
✓ When Social Services will return the telephone call

✓ What next year's fees will be
✓ How to deal with a plumbing problem in the toilets
✓ If the lunch has wheat in it

... and a multitude of other things from strategic decisions to minute detail. You will suddenly be expected to know all these things because you are the manager.

Most team members will be reasonable, of course. They will be just as patient as you were when someone else was your new manager and you needed support or information or a decision – that is probably only for a short period of time!

This 'magic dust' phenomenon is even more pronounced when you move to a new team or setting. Your new team only ever know you as a manager. To them you have no previous role as a practitioner without formal managerial responsibilities. You have no shared history that you can remind them of or that helps explain why you are still learning the ways of management. This fresh start can, however, work in your favour, as any of your previous mistakes are also not part of your new team's shared history.

A testing time

Whether you are promoted from within or appointed as a manager new to the service, your team members will soon want to know what sort of manager you are going to be.

Preparation and planning, based upon your values, will help you. Waiting until you are in a situation and then reacting will only result in your day being full of unforeseen challenges. How well you do will probably be more to do with instinct or luck than good management.

> 'People say that I'm lucky. But the more I practise the luckier I become.'

This quote is attributed to top 1960s professional golfer Gary Player. It illustrates the need to keep practising. No one who is good at something started off as an expert. Their skill needs to be practised. Mistakes need to be made. The learning that takes place following these mistakes helps to improve performance the next time.

Preparation will help you to demonstrate to your team your clear actions based upon priorities and values. The actions you take will let staff know what sort of manager you are.

BEING PREPARED

Use some of that symbolic 'magic dust' and shake it over yourself. Think about potential challenges that may happen tomorrow, or next week. What are your options? Who else could help? What are your likely actions? Like most good performers learning from the past and thinking about future actions will help you as a manager.

It is not only your team members who will expect things of you from the start. Other professionals will also need you to immediately take the responsibilities of being a manager.

ACTIVITY 2.7

Identify a range of other people who will need to recognise you in your managerial role.

_____

_____

_____

_____

Comment

Depending upon your setting you may have included:

❑ Your line manager
❑ Ofsted inspection team
❑ Social workers
❑ Health visitors
❑ Suppliers
❑ Bank manager
❑ Parents
❑ NVQ Centre staff

❑ Local authority, e.g. environmental health team
❑ College tutor
❑ Speech therapist
❑ Physiotherapist
❑ Portage worker

Each of the people you identified will need different things from you. As the manager you will need to be clear what they need, and indeed what you want from them in return. As the manager you can gain much by developing positive working relationships with a whole range of people.

PUTTING THEORY INTO PRACTICE

Whose views are important?

Getting good quality, constructive feedback is vital to your development process. To know how far you have to go; you need to know how far you have come already.

Developing the skill of seeking and obtaining feedback is one that you will benefit from.

There are many people who will have a view of your management style and skills. You will receive unsolicited feedback from some quarters. Ofsted will inspect when it's right for their agenda and timescale, not yours. Some parents, children and staff will tell you how they feel about your management when it is their 'right time'. This feedback may be positive and reassuring for you. It may, however, contain things that you don't agree with or that you believe to be untrue.

ACTIVITY 2.8

This activity would make an interesting scenario to role play with your mentor or a trusted colleague. Alternatively, you could work through it in your imagination.

Put yourself in the position of a manager who is receiving some negative feedback about some action you have taken. This might be related to the effect on staff or parents, for example. Someone who is unhappy or confused about the decision made tells you about how they feel. This conversation might be in a quiet place (such as an office) or in an open space (the reception area, or even the local supermarket).

Consider these questions.

❑ What would you say?
❑ How would you say it?
❑ How would you feel?
❑ Are the views of this person important?

Comment

This type of situation is difficult for most people. Few managers relish confrontation or receiving negative feedback. The skill in dealing with it is worth developing. What you say in response is important. Even more vital is that you listen to the comments. You can then decide whether the venue is the right one to respond (in the supermarket?) and what to say to demonstrate that you have heard and will respond. As important as what you say is how you say it.

How you say it will be strongly influenced by whether you believe the person's view is important.

If they have a stake in your Early Years service, then their view has an importance. It is therefore worth maintaining your professional approach (even in the supermarket) and controlling any adverse emotional reaction to enable you to sift through their comments and find the potential learning for yourself and your service.

'ON DUTY' EVEN WHEN YOU'RE NOT AT WORK

Brave enough to ask

If you wait long enough people will tell you some of what they think about your management style. However, good managers want to know. This information is usually available, always useful and provides you for free what a management consultant would charge you for.

IT IS OFTEN BETTER TO ASK THAN TO BE TOLD

Management Health Warning
Unless you are prepared to listen, DON'T ASK.

It will usually lead to a breakdown in working relationships if, motivated by feelings of obligation, you ask for feedback about your management practice.

Just because someone says that something is 'good' for you is not reason enough to try it.

Having said that, the learning you can achieve from positive, supportive criticism is immense, i.e. what is good and not so good about your management practice.

Remember that learning is not always pain-free. Therefore choose the time, place and circumstances to receive feedback.

You may not want to know about everything –

'Tell me what you thought of the way I handled that interview.'

You may value the views of some people over others –

'As my mentor, please give me feedback about my Inspection action plan.'

There are a variety of ways to ask for feedback. Depending upon your favoured styles and methods of communication you could choose to

❏ Invite people to discuss their views in private conversations at work
❏ Select a sample of people from a group whose views you seek and start a discussion about the service and your management
❏ Construct a questionnaire with choices of closed answers (yes or no) that encourages responses to specific things you want to know about
❏ Use a management framework such as the NVQ to ask for comments and/or ratings of your current practice.

These ideas can be developed to suit you and your situation. The important point is that listening to the views of other people will provide you with useful information to add to your self-perception.

The answer to the question 'How well am I doing as an Early Years manager?' will be complex. It is vital to ask it and valuable to compare different perspectives.

Remember that the views of others need to be evaluated. What weight you give to them will be your decision. Don't be flattered into complacency or demoralised into defeat.

Keep in touch with your roots and be kind to yourself

Take a moment to remember why you entered the world of Early Years.

During the career of most managers there will be times when the lack of change that you can see is vital, will frustrate you, annoy you and even anger you. Your job is to be ahead of the game, to be shaping the service for next week, next month and next year. The sense of urgency is good to have.

Remember the rest of the team and the other people around you. Change is a wonderful thing – as long as you are in control of it!

The values that you hold and believe in are part of what will continue to make you a good Early Years practitioner and manager.

As you develop more confidence and knowledge in your management skills and practice you may want others to follow your lead faster. You may have unrealistic expectations of them or yourself.

The point is to have *the* big aim for your service, have the ambition and drive to set challenging objectives. Remember, however, that real change takes time, and while the contribution of others may delay things it can help to achieve more in the long run.

As well as evaluating the movement towards objectives don't forget to celebrate the small successes and achievement of goals along the way.

Managing yourself – from colleague to boss

This chapter will have worked well if you are now feeling clearer about the changes, both personal and

THE LONGEST JOURNEY STARTS WITH A SINGLE STEP

professional, that you are involved in as a manager in Early Years.

The transition from being a team member to team leader is demanding and challenging. The expectations you place upon yourself will be accompanied by those expectations that others have of you within this role.

With a clearer internal view of yourself as the manager you are now ready to plan the next phase of your development in more detail.

REVIEW OF 'FROM COLLEAGUE TO BOSS'

This chapter has helped you if you can

✓ Feel comfortable thinking about yourself as a manager working within the Early Years sector

✓ Be prepared to recognise others in your team as more expert than you are in some areas of childcare practice
✓ Describe the benefits for you of having a mentor
✓ Outline some of the expectations that others have of you as a manager
✓ Plan ways to seek out and positively deal with critical feedback

References and suggested further reading

C. Kennedy (1991) *Guide to the Management Gurus*, Century Business.
N. Kline (1999) *Time to Think*, Ward Lock.

Website

www.early-years-nto.org.uk/NVQ4.pdf (provides the NVQ framework information)

Chapter 3

THE NEXT 100 DAYS

This chapter covers:

- Moving from ideas to action
- Methods of planning to support your development
- A framework to guide your continued professional development as an early years manager

---

SCENARIO CASE STUDY

'How is that new job going?' asked Kim.

When Jasmin thought about the question she realised that the job wasn't that new any more. She knew she'd been very busy over the last few months, but what had actually been achieved?

---

100 DAYS

Why 100 days? One hundred days, or three months, is traditionally a review period applied to new Prime Ministers. It is enough time, it is felt, for new policies to be evaluated in terms of change. Judgements are made as to what improvements or change have actually happened as a result of the new administration and approaches.

Within the management of an Early Years setting the same period of time seems reasonable to use to review your progress as a manager.

Every service will have an annual cycle that can be used to measure trends, such as occupancy rates, income & expenditure, and progress of children. This 100-day rule helps to focus attention on shorter stages that make up those annual measures.

Within the context of your development and practice as an Early Years manager the next three months is a short enough period to be at the forefront of your thinking and long enough to be able to recognise improvement (or not) as a result of changes made.

GETTING STARTED

Having a clear idea about what you want to achieve is a good starting-point. Although this may sound obvious it is not always easy to achieve. Sometimes we fall to the temptation to leave out the completion of this stage. Such an omission inevitably results in later frustration and disappointment. You can't know you have arrived if you don't know where you are going.

What you want to do

You are now invited to be self-centred, to think about yourself for some time. This is not something that most people practise frequently in a positive and empowered way. It is suggested that you read through this section in a place and time where you feel comfortable and uninterrupted, or reread it in such a context later.

Consider yourself in terms of your own management development over the next 100 days.

To help you with this broad request you may find the next activity useful.

ACTIVITY 3.1

In a relaxing time and place imagine that time has flown by and it is now three months in the future. Identify the date (make sure you are at work), the day, where you are and the time of day.

Imagine the weather, some of the smells and sounds of the environment you are in.

What are you doing and how are you demonstrating good management approaches and practice?

In your mind's eye see yourself coping, being proactive, in control and comfortable as a manager.

From the same point in the future imagine you are reflecting back over the 'past' 100 days. Identify significant events or planned activities related to work. These might include:

- ❏ festival celebrations
- ❏ routine functions
- ❏ staffing issues, e.g. recruitment or appraisals
- ❏ business decisions, e.g. budget or fee-setting
- ❏ crisis management, e.g. unexpected challenges such as complaints, disciplinary investigations or prolonged under-occupancy.

For each of these you dealt with their opportunities and challenges in a positive way. Identify how you applied your management skills to achieve this. You may have used previous experience, researched new ideas or asked for and received help from others.

Note down the main sets of skills and knowledge you 'used' in this period.

_____

_____

_____

_____

_____

_____

_____

Comment

This way of projecting into the future and then looking back uses techniques explained in ideas of Future Basing, and Neuro Linguistic Programming (NLP). It may at first feel strange, but the benefit of using such an approach is to start from an expectation of success. Rather than setting objectives for the future that look daunting and difficult you are encouraged to assume achievement and success and from such a position to consider how obstacles were overcome and success finally achieved. It is the difference between looking up to the top of the steep hill from the approach road, and from looking back down the hill acknowledging your achievement and celebrating the brilliant way you avoided the cowpats or thorn bushes. From the top you can also enjoy the view and remember why you ever wanted to climb the hill in the first place.

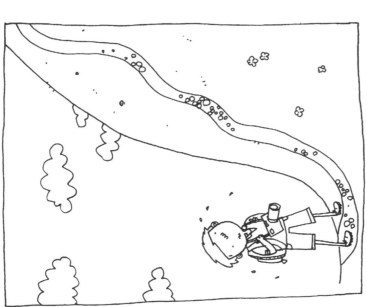

The starting-point really is to allow yourself to think across the broad range of your development as a manager. Bring together a collection of ideas that you would consider to be desirable. This is wishing time.

'As a manager I wish I were better at...'

This really is self-centred luxury. All these pages of thinking just about yourself, with no interruptions!

ACTIVITY 3.2

Note down your wish list of things that you would love to improve upon as a manager.

_____

_____

_____

_____

What is possible to do

Give your ideas a reality check. Anyone can dream, but now continues the serious business of getting to action and improvements.

Think about the next three months in practical terms. What do you know is going to happen to take up your energy and focus? These things may be major events or activities in your working life, or in your personal life. Take into account this awareness and the probable effects upon you. You will need to keep these pressures in mind when working out objectives for your continual development plan (see below).

As well as events there are other factors that may well determine the successful completion of your objectives. Depending upon the final choices you make, such factors could include resources, equipment, finances or other people.

If you need other people to support you or to cooperate with your planned objectives you should consider the possibilities of these people being in the right place, time and frame of mind.

One of the skills of the manager is to remember when constructing any plan that wherever people are involved things will probably take twice as long as you plan for at first. This is not a disparaging slur on 'everyone else'. It is recognition that, especially in service sectors such as Early Years, change and understanding take time. A process of embracing change goes through stages and takes some time. These stages can include:

❏ denial that things need to change
❏ awareness that things need to change
❏ producing a number of ideas for change
❏ testing different ideas for change
❏ deciding upon the most appropriate ideas
❏ planning to implement the change
❏ explaining the implementation to other key people
❏ implementing change
❏ reviewing the outcomes.

While this list may set out a linear and logical process, many managers don't plan to address each stage at a conscious level. Therefore, when the manager introduces and explains something to staff for the first time they will already have gone through many of the previous stages.

For the staff (or anyone else) listening to you it is the first time they have heard it. All those questions and ways of exploring the issues until the conclusion was reached that this was the best way forward will go through the minds of the listening audience. When such exploratory questions are raised it is easy for a manager to hear them as blocks or negative criticisms. Often they are not.

ACTIVITY 3.3

For ideas you noted down in the previous activity think about the resources and people you would need to achieve improvements. Try giving a priority rating to each idea chosen in light of the resources identified. If something is one of your top priorities you could allocate an A rating, medium priority a B rating, and so on.

_____

_____

_____

_____

Comment

The rating system you use is not as important as the act of starting to prioritise your wish list within a real context. Before moving on just check that you have not prioritised a whole career's worth of development, remember this is for the next 100 days.

Your priority – first things first

Many things are desirable. Some things are possible, at a cost. The next step is to consider what to choose as the top priorities for the next three months.

When faced with alternatives some people choose the easiest first. The feeling of getting off to a good start, of doing something that you know you can achieve, is a positive motivator.

'Try eating your chips first. I know you love them. After that you can try the broccoli.'

Other people favour tackling the thing that most daunts them, or that offers the largest challenge. The easier things then act as a kind of reward.

'After we have tidied away all those toys we can have a story.'

There is no correct way of going about this. Whatever works for you is right.

ACTIVITY 3.4

Reflect upon your list and your ratings.

You can now consider what your order of priority is for the next 100 days.

Top priority should be that area of your management that, if you cannot achieve anything else, is the one that you will consider a good step in the right direction.

Stop prioritising areas whenever you feel that your realistic expectations have been reached – that

> even if everything goes to plan that is all that is achievable in the time. Other areas of development can, of course, be carried forward to later times.

PLAN AHEAD

Planning in a context

Think about yourself as a manager in a concentrated and honest way.

Over the next 100 days you will change.

Opportunities will present themselves or be available to be found.

Challenges will arise.

You can wait to react and respond to whatever working life throws at you *or* you can have some clear

PLOT YOUR COURSE

landmarks in mind and plot a course towards where you want to go.

In terms of your management development you will already have some clear priorities. Before committing these to yourself in writing it may be beneficial to check them against some useful frameworks.

Using the Adair model (see Chapter 1) you can check which area your priorities cover:

Task – an aspect of the service for children or parents
Team – something to benefit teamwork
Individual – address the needs of a least one team member's performance.

The NVQ framework[1] includes relevant units about how you 'Develop your own resources' (MCI C2). This provides a model to check on:

Communication – getting feedback from others about your performance as a manager
Competence – knowing what skills and practices your job requires of you and how to measure them
Context – thinking about expectations of your job now and over the forthcoming period
Training & development – knowing your own needs and having a plan to address them.

Another part of that unit offers these points as a further checklist:

Delegation – what to delegate and how to support others

[1] NVQ in Early Years Care & Education Level 4.

Information handling – using data to inform decision-making

Monitoring & evaluating – knowing its importance and how to do it

Planning – developing the skills to construct an achievable action plan

Time management – planning time and minimising interruptions.

Setting objectives

In the same way as you had to learn and get used to Early Years jargon, the specific vocabulary of management is also worth becoming familiar with. One of the areas of confusion and uncertainty in 'management speak' is the use of 'objective' and 'goal'. Unfortunately different theorists and models use the words to mean slightly different things. In this series of books the following definition is used.

Objective = a statement outlining an intended and measurable series of actions towards a defined outcome.

An objective provides a clear framework to help you to achieve planned change. It should be

✓ Specific
✓ Measurable
✓ Achievable
✓ Resourced
✓ and over a defined Timescale.

Often the mnemonic SMART is used as a reminder of these five characteristics. Remembering them is the easy part. Many people find it hard to apply the five rules to constructing objectives. This is a skill worth developing. It will help you in many aspects of your management, for example when managing yourself, other people in your team, or projects.

SCENARIO CASE STUDY

Bobbie was really pleased with how last week's meeting had gone with Kyle. As the newest member of the team, Kyle had been keen to take on the organisation of the Noah's Ark nursery's first anniversary party for children and parents.

The press were arriving for the pre-party publicity photographs in 15 minutes. Bobbie would just check with Kyle that she didn't need any last-minute help.

MEETING OF MINDS

By developing the practice of defining SMART objectives you can improve on the ways that you explain your expectations to team members and so avoid misunderstandings. Clear objectives also provide you with a strong framework to measure progress and the effectiveness of work.

ACTIVITY 3.5

Read through the following statement and check to decide which are SMART objectives.

❑ Jay needs to improve her motivation, immediately.
❑ By next Tuesday you need to have the final report in the post to the social worker.
❑ To avoid a financial problem we need either to cut back on spending or to increase our fees.
❑ To meet parents' expectations each keyworker will produce a written report about their child every 6 weeks.

Comment

Use the 5-point mnemonic (SMART) to review these. To meet the test they would need to be specific, measurable in outcome and over a clear timescale – so that you could make a judgement that the outcome has been achieved. To be achievable and resourced you may have to make some assumptions in these examples.

To help you practise this seemingly simple, yet often difficult skill, try using this framework to write some of your own objectives.

Specific Measurable Achievable Resourced	Timed
Present the completed Post-inspection action plan to the full staff team through a presentation and with written copies for each person	*By 15th January*

Objective 1

Specific Measurable Achievable Resourced	Timed

Objective 2

Specific Measurable Achievable Resourced	Timed

Objective 3

Specific Measurable Achievable Resourced	Timed

Goal-setting

Having now practised the art of objective-setting you will find this part easy. Earlier it was established that the word objective was used to mean 'a statement outlining an intended and measurable series of actions towards a defined outcome'.

Each objective can be broken into action steps required to achieve the objective. These steps, or goals, are the practical things that need to happen, often in a certain order, to get into a position to achieve the objective fully.

For example, if my objective is to

> *Present the completed Post-inspection action plan to the full staff team through a presentation and with written copies for each person by 15th January*

I need to complete a number of goals to work up to the achievement as defined.

Goals to reach in this example might include:

- ❑ Analyse the inspection report to identify required or desired actions
- ❑ Prioritise these actions within the context of the setting
- ❑ Identify possible staff members to be responsible for each action (including *self*)
- ❑ Identify realistic and acceptable timescales for each outcome
- ❑ Identify required resources
- ❑ Write up the Post-inspection action plan in draft ready for the staff meeting
- ❑ Share the staff meeting agenda in good time
- ❑ Decide upon the most appropriate method of presenting this within the staff meeting.

This set of goals may be produced in the form of a 'To do' list that is written in sequential order – first things first.

Continued Professional Development (CPD)

The next 100 days are important to you because they are the *next* days in your development.

If you set yourself objectives to improve your skills,

knowledge or managerial practice then you will have made a good start. When you achieve these objectives you should celebrate your success.

However, don't mistake progress for finishing.

These objectives have been the next steps in your development. Your longer-scale development can be described within your Continued Professional Development (CPD) plan.

As an Early Years practitioner you are familiar with professional updating and reflective practice. This should also be applied to your managerial role.

Preparing a CPD plan
By reflecting upon your thinking and the activities completed in this book you will be able to answer the following questions:

❑ What is your present range of managerial skills, knowledge and practice as required by your job role?
❑ What are your main strengths as an Early Years manager?
❑ What are the main areas of improvement you have?
❑ Do you have the required experience or qualifications for your current job?
❑ Do you have an expectation of new demands or opportunities in your near future?

Once you have decided upon your answers to these questions you can complete a CPD review and plan. The pro-forma opposite is an example of how this can be recorded.

The discipline and effort of writing your CPD plan will be worthwhile. It will help you to focus upon your skills

Continued Professional Development
Review & Plan

Name:_____ Current post:_____
Management qualifications:_____

	Strengths	Improvement Areas
People		
Finance		
Communication		
Resources		
Other		

CPD Objectives:

Review Methods & Dates:

and identify objectives that mean the most to you. It is also great practice for helping your staff team to work on their CPD development.

Plans into action
Once you have identified the objectives you will then list the goals to act upon.

The act of writing down your development objectives is really important. In the same way as writing down agreements with team members, parents and Ofsted inspectors is important as a method of clarification and certainty, your 'contract' with yourself is more likely to be kept.

Be strict with the review dates. Make a note in your diary for the future dates to check on progress.

REVIEW OF 'THE NEXT 100 DAYS'

This chapter has helped you if you can

✓ Describe the main management areas that you plan to develop for yourself over the next few months
✓ Outline a process for deciding on what to do, how to do it and how to review progress.

References and suggested further reading

R. Bandler and J. Grinder (1979) *Frogs into Princes: Neuro Linguistic Programming*, Eden Grove.
A. Dickson (1983) *A Woman in Your Own Right: Assertiveness and You*, Quartet.
N. Kline (1999) *Time to Think*, Ward Lock.

Websites

www.instepuk.com (for information on Future Basing)
www.nlpinfo.com (for an introduction to and information about
Neuro Linguistic Programming (NLP))

REVIEW OF *SELF-DEVELOPMENT FOR EARLY YEARS MANAGERS*

This book has aimed to focus your attention on you. The introduction of a management context was provided to support your development over the next months and beyond. The success of the service that you manage is directly connected with your own development and success.

Even in the demanding world of Early Years provision you should make time to develop yourself as a manager.

Many people are depending upon you to do a good job.

You are worth the time and effort – invest in yourself.

INDEX